Paul Barrow

First published 1997

ISBN 0 7110 2400 6

© The National Railway Museum 1997

Published by Ian Allan Publishing

an imprint of Ian Allan Ltd, Terminal House, Station Approach,
Shepperton, Surrey TW17 8AS.
Printed by Ian Allan Printing Ltd, at its works at Coombelands
in Runnymede, England

Code: 9704/B2

IAN ALLAN
Publishing

Front cover: LNER 'A4' 4-6-2 No 60022 *Mallard* awaits
departure from Grantham with an express to King's Cross
from Leeds and Bradford in 1962.
Colour-Rail BRE688

Back cover: In its distinctive blue livery *Deltic*
heads an up express away from Askham Tunnel in
June 1959. The locomotive was displayed in the
Science Museum from 1963 until October 1993
when it was moved to York.
Colour-Rail DE574

This page: A view from the footplate of *Mallard*
at 70mph. *NRM/P. Ransome-Wallis collection*

Great British Locomotives
Michael Blakemore and David Mosley

NATIONAL
mm
RAILWAY
MUSEUM

Locomotives in Action

Introduction

When putting together this book on the locomotives of the National Railway Museum 'in action', our thoughts were initially to show them in what might be described as their 'heyday'. But when *was* the heyday of the locomotives which make up the most extensive single collection of steam, diesel and electric locomotives in Britain? Was it when they travelled the nation's railway system doing the work for which they were built, or is it today, when they stand splendidly restored in museum condition or perhaps occasionally operating on one of the preserved railways?

When looking at the locomotives as they are today, it is sometimes difficult to realise that they now enjoy a special status which, by and large, they never had during their working lives. To the railway companies which owned them they were merely the units of traction which hauled their passengers and freight — the tools of their trade — and few were regarded as anything 'special'. The reasons for the choice of the locomotives which constitute the National Collection are too diverse to discuss here but in many cases it comes down to no more than being the first example or last survivor of a notable class or a typical representative of a significant type.

In only a few instances did a locomotive acquire a special status during its active life and that was due to its association with a particular event. The best example of that is the LNER 'A4' 4-6-2 No 4468 *Mallard*, whose place in the collection (as opposed to any other example of the class) is owed to its achievement of a world speed record for steam traction in 1938. But this is where history throws up odd quirks of fate! At the time, no great ceremony was made of that record run; after all, it was but the latest in a series of record runs during the 1930s. What, though, if *Mallard's* record had been beaten (and, had it not been for the outbreak of war, it almost certainly would have been), who would remember *Mallard* today? It might well have been another member of the class — the first built or the last in service — which represented 1930s streamlining in the Collection and not world record breaking! Another example of a locomotive which gained celebrity as a result of its involvement with a particular event is the Southern Railway 'Battle of Britain' class 4-6-2 No 34051 *Winston Churchill*. A representative of this controversial design was scheduled for preservation in the Collection but it was the occasion of Sir Winston Churchill's state funeral, when the train was hauled by the locomotive named after him, that identified the selected candidate.

In only a very few cases can it be said that a locomotive has been destined for the National Collection from the outset of its career; perhaps that can only really be said of No 92220 *Evening Star*, the last steam locomotive built by British Railways. Since the decision to cease building steam locomotives had been taken several years earlier, it was known that the final member of the last batch to be built would be the last of all and its place in the Collection was thus always assured.

So, then, for most of the National Collection, the heyday is really *now*, when the happenstance of preservation has elevated a diverse collection of machines from being mainly unconsidered workhorses to polished and valued treasures which, taken together, trace the story of railway motive power in Britain.

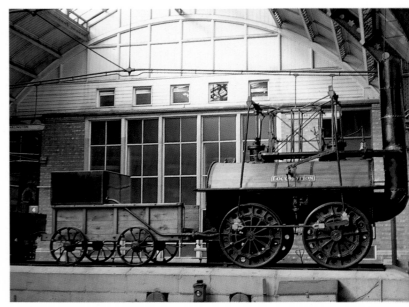

Stockton & Darlington Railway 0-4-0 *Locomotion* (1825)
Above: Preservation 'just the way it was' with a priceless artefact on an unprotected plinth. *Locomotion* is seen here at Darlington Bank Top station in 1967; the locomotive is now in the North Road Station Museum at Darlington. *J. S. Gilks*

The locomotives which constitute the National Collection have arrived from a variety of inheritances, but it is a sad fact that many types worthy of representation went for scrap before their historical significance came to be appreciated and before the saving of important examples came to be regarded as worthwhile. The first acquisitions came to the Science Museum via the Commissioners of Patents, but the first museum specifically devoted to railways was opened in York by the LNER in 1927. Several railways had the foresight to set a number of locomotives aside for preservation (though, regrettably, a few were subsequently scrapped) but after Nationalisation the British Transport Commission pursued a formal policy of securing a collection of railway artefacts of all descriptions, not the least being locomotives considered of particular importance. Under the British Railways Board (successor to the BTC) new museums were opened at Clapham and Swindon in the 1960s, although the locomotive collection continued to grow as steam locomotives were withdrawn and many examples remained in storage. The transfer of the collections to the Department of Education & Science as a result of the 1968 Transport Act saw the opening of a new National Railway Museum in York in 1975, based in the former York North motive power depot. This brought together the collections previously housed in the Clapham and old York museums, to which the NRM was able to add new acquisitions from elsewhere, including locomotive classes still then in use on BR. Nevertheless, the locomotive collection has always been too large for it all to be housed at York and items can be seen on loan to other museums or preserved railways at many locations throughout the country.

In choosing the illustrations for this book we have tried to show as many of the locomotives as we could and, wherever possible, as they were when at work in regular service. Some have escaped us, either because their working days were over before the advent of colour photography or simply because they eluded the photographers whose work has been available to us. Not every one of the photographs, it must be admitted, shows the locomotives 'in action' in the strictest sense of the word and there are a few which illustrate locomotives not actually at work but at an interesting stage of their 'non-working' careers. A considerable number of locomotives, however, have operated on the main lines, on preserved railways or on the Museum site and so we have also included a representative selection of these to show that the National Railway Museum has, from the beginning, been very much a working museum.

The illustrations have been arranged in chronological order of date of building and this enables us to show that many examples of what are often referred to as 'modern' traction (ie diesel and electric) are, in fact, older than some of the steam locomotives. It also allows us to close the book with a special category of museum locomotive — the modern working reproduction. Here, then, is the National Railway Museum's locomotive collection at work.

Furness Railway 0-4-0 No 3 (1846)

Above: Furness Railway No 3, affectionately and hardly surprisingly nicknamed *Coppernob*, is one of two survivors of a large number of locomotives built by the firm of Bury, Curtis & Kennedy in the formative years of main line railways. The locomotive has bar-frames and the hemispherical firebox characteristic of Bury's designs.

Coppernob served the Furness faithfully until December 1898 when it was withdrawn and retained for preservation. In the summer of 1901 the locomotive was placed in a glass pavilion on the station at Barrow-in-Furness. The pavilion was destroyed in the air-raid of the night of 4/5 May 1941, but *Coppernob* was largely intact and was removed to Horwich for safekeeping. The locomotive formed part of the display at Clapham from 1962-1975 and on 21 April 1975 arrived at York.

In the summer of 1996 *Coppernob* revisited the Furness peninsula to 'star' in the celebrations for the 150th anniversary of the Furness Railway. The locomotive is seen here on the former Lakeside branch, now the Lakeside & Haverthwaite Railway, in August 1996. *Peter van Zeller*

Acknowledgements

We would like to record our thanks to Phil Atkins of the National Railway Museum for his assistance in compiling the historical notes, to Jane Elliott, Sheila Granger and Debbie Heron for their transcription skills, and to all the photographers for their foresight in recording the scenes featured in this book.

M. Blakemore
D. W. Mosley
January 1997

London & North Western Railway 0-4-0ST No 1439 (1865)

Left: This is probably one of the least known of the National Collection locomotives. Its history is a fascinating one which illustrates well the role of chance and longevity in the survival of locomotives.

No 1439 was one of 36 '4ft shunters' built to the design of John Ramsbottom at Crewe. The locomotive has a cylindrical firebox similar in style to the type used by Ramsbottom for the narrow gauge engines at Crewe Works. It was sold to ICI in Birmingham in 1919 for a handsome price of £1,300 and was reboilered by Bagnall's in 1935, that firm having embraced boilers with cylindrical fireboxes for a number of its designs. The locomotive was donated to the British Transport Commission in 1954. Mr R. C. Bond, BTC Chief Officer (Mechanical Engineering), received the locomotive and 'proceeded — in no uncertain manner — to drive the locomotive to its new ownership' (*Engineering*, 18 June 1954). *NRM collection*

Great Northern Railway 4-2-2 No 1 (1870)

Left: In early and mid-Victorian times loco designers favoured big driving wheels for passenger locomotives; in fact, large wheels were necessary for high speeds given the engineering standards of the day in terms of pistons, valve gear and coupling rods. GNR No 1 epitomises the classic single wheeler with its 8ft driving wheels. Built in 1870 and now enjoying its 90th year in preservation, No 1 was returned to steam in 1938 by the LNER for publicity purposes in connection with the introduction of its new rolling stock for the 'Flying Scotsman' service and on 24 August worked from King's Cross to Cambridge with a train of six-wheeled carriages (still then in use!) to show the style of the train of 50 years earlier. The special was photographed near Brookmans Park. Although the quality of this picture is not that of others in this book, it is one of the 'red-letter' days in railway preservation, being the oldest picture of a Museum engine in action. *Colour-Rail NE78*

Right: In the early 1980s No 1 was returned to steam once again at the NRM and visited both the Great Central and North Yorkshire Moors Railways. It is shown here on the latter line at Levisham during a BBC *Open University* filming assignment in October 1985. *NRM collection*

London & South Western Railway 2-4-0WT No 30587 (1874)

Above: The LSWR 2-4-0 well tanks of W. G. Beattie (a well tank has a small tank for water between its frames) is one of the National Collection's most remarkable survivors. A total 85 locomotives of this design were built between 1863 and 1875 for use on London suburban services and on branch lines. However, by the early 1880s the increasing weight of trains was exceeding the capacity of the well tanks and withdrawal of the class — with three exceptions — had occurred by 1898.

In Cornwall the branch from Wadebridge to Bodmin and Wenford Bridge, which carried china clay, required locomotives with a light axle-loading and short wheelbase to negotiate its sharp curves. The Beattie well tanks proved curiously suitable for this branch and thus three engines survived for another 60 years; despite the disappearance of the rest of the class before the end of the 19th century, they defied all efforts to find satisfactory replacements until 1962! No 30587 takes water in Pencarrow Woods with the branch freight in April 1961. The locomotive is currently displayed in LSWR livery as No 298 in the South Devon Railway's museum at Buckfastleigh.
Colour-Rail BRS498

Above: After the end of its duties at Wadebridge in September 1962, No 30587 returned to London to make two final runs on 2 and 16 December on enthusiasts' specials from Waterloo to Shepperton and Hampton Court, double-heading with 'sister' engine No 30585. It is seen here by the coaling tower at Nine Elms depot. *NRM/M. D. England collection*

London & North Western Railway 'Precedent' class 2-4-0 No 790 *Hardwicke* (1892)

Above: Hardwicke represents the stuff of railway legend. The locomotive was the star of the West Coast running during the dramatic interlude of the 'Races to the North' in the summer of 1895, running 19 of the 35 racing legs between Crewe and Carlisle. On 22 August, the final night of the Races, *Hardwicke* ran the 141 miles from Crewe to Carlisle including the arduous climb over Shap in 126min, an average speed of 67.2mph with a maximum of 82mph at Wreay, a mere five miles out of Carlisle.

F. W. Webb, the designer of the 'Precedents', was more renowned for his experiments with compound propulsion but the 'Precedents' were a small, simple and robust design. Although constructed as a new loco in 1892, *Hardwicke* was regarded by the LNWR as a replacement for an earlier engine built in 1873 and so carries that year as its building date.

Hardwicke was eventually withdrawn from LMS service in January 1932. The locomotive was restored to LNWR livery and stored in the paint shop at Crewe until 1962 when it was placed in the Clapham Museum. It was restored to working order at Carnforth in 1974 and featured in both the Shildon and Rainhill celebrations. The locomotive, in company with the ex-LNWR Royal Train Brake No 5155, is seen here at Dringhouses, York, on a test-run prior to the latter event.
NRM collection

Great Eastern Railway Class T26 2-4-0 No 490 (1894)

Above: The Great Eastern 'T26' class, commonly known as 'Intermediates', was unusual in that the locomotives were designed for mixed duties on secondary lines. The more usual procedure was to cascade down ageing express locomotives for lighter duties.

Classified 'E4' by the LNER and renumbered No 7490, the locomotive seems to have led a largely anonymous existence, although in 1930 it appeared at Nottingham Victoria complete with a seat on the buffer beam. This fitting was apparently for the judges of the local station gardens competition — for the most uninterrupted of views!

The locomotive was withdrawn from service in 1959, entered the Clapham Museum in 1962 and came to York in 1975. It is at present on display at Bressingham, Norfolk. The photograph of No 62785 (BR number) was taken at Haverhill in April 1958. All the fittings of the rural railway are still evident and the occasion is the annual Cambridge University Railway Club engine-driving day, which by this time usually featured a veteran locomotive such as an 'E4'. Of purely museum interest is the third figure from the left striding towards the camera, an undergraduate J. A. Coiley — later first 'Keeper' (as it was then termed) of the National Railway Museum. *R. C. Riley*

Great Western Railway 'Dean Goods' 0-6-0 No 2516 (1897)

Above: The 0-6-0 goods engine was the most numerous type in the country and earned railways their 'bread and butter' for over a century. A notable example is the 'Dean Goods' 0-6-0 No 2516 seen here at the Oswestry depot in 1952; five years into Nationalisation the initials 'GWR' are still visible on the tender. These locomotives were strong and efficient and were also put to good use on branch line passenger work. With 59 years' service to its credit, No 2516 is displayed in the Great Western Railway Museum at Swindon. *Colour-Rail BRW635*

Great Northern Railway 4-4-2s
Nos 990 *Henry Oakley* (1898) and 251 (1902)

Above: The railways had been served well by 4-4-0s but as bigger boilers and fireboxes became necessary to handle heavier trains, 4-4-2 and 4-6-0 wheel arrangements were adopted. The first 4-4-2 (or Atlantic) was GNR No 990 *Henry Oakley* in 1898 and in 1902 a larger version with wide firebox was introduced, of

which No 251 was the first. No 990 had been placed in the old York Railway Museum by the LNER, which also set No 251 aside for preservation in 1947, both being restored to GNR livery, but in 1953 the pair returned to steam for a special train from London King's Cross to Doncaster marking the centenary of Doncaster Works. The two Atlantics are here approaching their destination with the 'Plant Centenarian' on 27 September 1953. *Colour-Rail P169*

Left: Henry Oakley was the first loco to be steamed at the NRM and on 31 August 1975 ran in the 'Rail 150' cavalcade at Shildon celebrating the 150th anniversary of the Stockton & Darlington Railway. The GNR did not indulge in the naming of its locomotives and No 990 was very much the exception to the rule; it commemorates the company's long-serving General Manager from 1870 to 1898. *Hugh Ballantyne*

Below: In 1954 No 251 worked two special trains. It is here the focus of admiration at Edgehill, Liverpool, having worked in from Retford with the 'Northern Rubber Special'. On this day, 4 September, No 251 was assisted by Class D11 4-4-0 No 62663 *Prince Albert. Colour-Rail 590*

Midland Railway Locomotives

Above: Sentiment came a poor second to profit in the eyes of the old railway companies. Preservation of redundant locomotives was a low priority and even locomotives which had been set aside for posterity sometimes disappeared in the frenzy of progress. Both Derby and Swindon Works in their time were guilty of cutting up what today would be considered priceless items.

The Stockton & Darlington centenary celebrations of 1925 gave an impetus to preservation which was carried on with the establishment of the 'old' York Museum in 1927. In the 1950s the British Transport Commission established a Department of Historical Relics and the future of many casually preserved locomotives was assured. Between 1958 and 1961 the Commission advisory panel drew up a list of locomotives to be officially preserved as the steam age ended.

This picture, taken at Derby in, we surmise, the summer of 1959, shows a part of this proto-National Collection. The locomotives are: (from left to right) MR 4-2-2 No 118 (now No 673) of 1899, LTSR 4-4-2T No 80 *Thundersley* (1909), MR Compound 4-4-0 No 1000 (1902) and MR 2-4-0 No 158A (1866). *Colour-Rail*

Midland Railway 4-2-2 No 673 (1899)

*Above:*The single-driver express locomotive, increasingly outclassed by four and six-wheeled types, enjoyed a brief revival at the turn of the century encouraged by the invention of steam sanding which allowed increased adhesion when starting a train or climbing a gradient.

One of the most elegant types, S. W. Johnson's 1899 design for the Midland Railway, was always referred to as 'Spinners' for the supposedly effortless way in which the locomotives spun along the tracks.

The National Collection locomotive, No 673, was withdrawn from service by the LMS in 1928 and set aside for preservation. In 1929 the locomotive was repainted in Midland livery and given its original number, No 118. It remained at Derby, making occasional appearances at open days and the like until transferred to the Midland Railway Centre at Butterley. Here the locomotive was restored to working order in its 1909 style with the appropriate chimney, livery and number, No 673.

No 673 ran in the 'Rocket 150' celebrations and is seen here, in the heart of Midland territory at Westhouses, en route to Rainhill on 21 May 1980. *Hugh Ballantyne*

London & South Western Railway 'T9' 4-4-0 No 120 (1899)

Above right: Introduced in 1899, the LSWR 'T9' proved to be one of that company's most useful passenger classes and No 120 of this type is currently on loan to the Bluebell Railway. When built, the 'T9s' were unsuperheated but from 1922 they began to be equipped with superheaters and extended smokeboxes, No 120 being so treated in 1927. As BR No 30120, it is shown here on a down passenger working at Eastleigh on 11 October 1958. *R. C. Riley*

Right: No 120 was selected for preservation in 1961 and the following year was repainted in LSWR livery. This was not actually accurate since it had been given an extended smokebox and superheating by the Southern Railway, a case which amply illustrates the perennial difficulty of matching the changing technical condition of a locomotive with a livery appropriate to it. In this guise No 120 was used for a couple of years on enthusiasts' excursions and occasional scheduled services, including the 12.42pm SO Waterloo–Basingstoke which it heads through Berrylands on 30 June 1962. *J. S. Gilks*

Great Northern Railway Class J13 0-6-0ST No 1247 (1899)

Above: This locomotive was presented to the National Collection in 1980 by Captain 'Bill' Smith. It thus became the first working steam locomotive to be donated to the Museum by a private individual.

No 1247 was built by Sharp Stewart & Co in Glasgow in 1899 to the designs of H. A. Ivatt. The locomotive spent most of its life in the London area where its duties included shunting, local freights and station pilot duties at King's Cross. The LNER reclassified the locomotive 'J52' and renumbered it No 4247 in 1924 and No 8846 in 1946. It finally became No 68846 under the nationalised British Railways in 1948.

The locomotive was repainted in the lined black livery as shown in the photograph in September 1958 and appeared, along with *Mallard*, at an exhibition to celebrate the 750th anniversary of the Borough of Wood Green in North London. No 68846 was purchased by Captain Smith in 1959, returned to Great Northern livery as No 1247 and commenced a career which involved, at first, main line steam tours (the first privately-owned locomotive to do so) and eventually running on several of the country's preserved railways. *R. C. Riley*

Above: Captain Smith presented No 1247 to the National Collection in 1980. The locomotive came into York from the North Yorkshire Moors Railway by road and finally by way of the Derwent Valley Light Railway, an agricultural branch line which wandered into the city from the East Riding. The locomotive is seen here at the Layerthorpe terminus of the DVLR in company with a Robert Stephenson & Hawthorn diesel shunter also destined for the National Collection.

No 1247 returned to steam in 1980 and has been used regularly for operational and demonstration purposes at the Museum. In 1991 the locomotive represented the Museum at the 10th anniversary celebrations of the California State Railroad Museum in Sacramento. At the time of writing the locomotive is on the East Somerset Railway where it has, once again, assumed its final railway service livery and guise as No 68846. *NRM collection*

South Eastern & Chatham Railway Class D 4-4-0 No 737 (1901)
London & South Western Railway Class T3 4-4-0 No 563 (1893)

Above: The 4-4-0 type was widely adopted in the later 19th century for express passenger work and the National Collection is particularly well endowed with 4-4-0s of both inside and outside cylinder varieties. Use of outside cylinders and motion enabled a longer firebox within a coupled wheelbase and made valve gear more accessible. Examples of both are seen in this interesting view on 31 January 1961 showing the Museum of British Transport at Clapham being set up. On the left is

SECR No 737, a simple but successful design and superbly arrayed in the most elaborate livery of any NRM locomotive. Behind it is LSWR No 563 receiving a repaint. No 563 was originally withdrawn in 1939 but the outbreak of war saw it reinstated to help with the great demands expected of the nation's railways. This reprieve was to earn its preservation for, although withdrawn in 1945, it had not been cut up by 1948 when it was repainted in LSWR livery for an exhibition to mark the centenary of Waterloo station. *R. C. Riley*

Midland Railway 4-4-0 No 1000 (1902)

Above: The Midland 'Compounds' were by far the most numerous class of three-cylinder compound locomotives built anywhere in the world. They were also the longest lasting of any British compound design and were the most successful, being fast and economical by the standards of their time.

Built at Derby as No 2631 in 1902, No 1000 was renumbered in 1907 and rebuilt into largely its present configuration with a superheated boiler in 1914. The locomotive was withdrawn from service in September 1951 and was stored at Derby

Works. No 1000 was returned to working order in 1959 and until 1962 ran as one of a pool of vintage locomotives along with, for example, *City of Truro* and *Gordon Highlander,* on enthusiasts' specials.

In December 1962 No 1000 was placed in the Museum of British Transport at Clapham and in 1975 transferred to York. The locomotive appeared at both Stockton & Darlington and Liverpool & Manchester 150th celebrations and has run on a number of main line specials. The picture shows the delightful clutter of the steam age at Derby Works in May 1959 as No 1000 is restored to working order. *R. C. Riley*

Above: These two pictures illustrate two widely differing aspects of a museum locomotive's activities.

This picture shows the Compound at Nottingham Midland station in September 1959, with the locomotive hauling a Stephenson Locomotive Society special from Birmingham and Derby. The transport policeman seems to have the crowd of stylishly dressed enthusiasts in order! *R. C. Riley*

Right: The picture opposite shows the locomotive with vintage LMS carriages at York station on 1 July 1981. The train was used as part of a television commercial for 'Ovaltine' biscuits — a product not as successful as the Compound itself! *NRM collection*

Great Western Railway 'City' class 4-4-0
No 3440 *City of Truro* (1903)

Above: Of the inside-cylinder 4-4-0s in the Collection, the best known is undoubtedly the GWR's No 3440 *City of Truro*. Under William Dean the GWR express fleet moved from the 4-2-2 wheel arrangement to a range of highly successful double-framed 4-4-0s and the 'Cities' were developed from the earlier 'Atbara' class of 1900 but with a larger boiler. No 3440's place in history is due to its epic performance on 9 May 1904 when it was credited with attaining 100mph down Wellington Bank, in Somerset, the first claimed speed of 100mph on rail. Although the speed has never been authenticated beyond dispute, there is no doubt that a very high speed was reached on that occasion. After withdrawal in 1931, the GWR arranged for the loco to be placed in the York Railway Museum where it remained until 1957. It was then removed for a period of further activity on special trains and occasional regular

services, notably on the Didcot, Newbury & Southampton line. Early in this phase of its career, *City of Truro* stands at Southampton Terminus on 29 June 1957.
R. C. Riley

Right: From 1962 to 1984 *City of Truro* resided in the GWR Museum at Swindon but then emerged yet again to be restored to working order for the 'GW 150' celebrations in 1985. After arriving back in the city in which it had first been preserved, No 3440 made a number of runs to Scarborough on the 'Scarborough Spa Express' trains and the veteran 4-4-0 is depicted with incongruous BR-liveried carriages near Kirkham Abbey on 31 August 1987. During this third spell of active life, it also visited the Netherlands for a month in 1989 for the 150th anniversary of that country's railways.
J. S. Gilks

North Eastern Railway Bo-Bo Electric No 1 (1904)

Above: Two locomotives of this type were built by the North Eastern Railway for the working of the steep and tortuous Quayside branch in Newcastle upon Tyne. Supplied by Brush Electrical Engineering subcontracting to British Thomson-Houston, they represented the first style of main line electric locomotive in Britain.

The locomotives led a leisurely existence on 'their' branch, working one week on and one week off. For the safety of the shunters working in the yards at each end of the branch, overhead pick-up equipment was provided. Through the narrow tunnels of the branch itself third-rail equipment was provided, current being supplied at 600V dc. Upon Nationalisation No 1 received the number 26500 and in June 1961, after repair, emerged in full North Eastern green livery. The photograph shows the locomotive in this condition at Heaton depot in July of the same year.

No 26500 was withdrawn from service in September 1964 and stored at South Gosforth. It escaped scrapping and was displayed at Leicester from 1968 to 1975. It was the only electric locomotive on display when the Museum opened in 1975 and is presently in NER livery. *Colour-Rail DE840*

Great Western Railway '28xx' 2-8-0 No 2818 (1905)

Above: The eight-coupled outside-cylinder freight locomotive, with small diameter driving wheels for maximum adhesion, first appeared as an 0-8-0 on the Barry Railway. With the increasing use of superheating, a pair of carrying wheels was added at the front to accommodate the extra weight and the 2-8-0 became the standard goods engine on three of the 'Big Four' companies before Nationalisation. The GWR '28xx' class was the first 2-8-0 type and is represented in the NRM by No 2818. It is seen here on 27 April 1963, four months before withdrawal, in typical latter-day goods engine condition somewhat off GW territory at Woodford Halse depot, on the Great Central main line, having worked in with a freight from the Western Region via Banbury.
R. C. Riley

Great Western Railway 'Star' class 4-6-0 No 4003 *Lode Star* (1907)

Above: The 'family' of Great Western four-cylinder 4-6-0s, 'Stars', 'Castles' and 'Kings' were some of the most significant locomotive designs in British railway history.

George Jackson Churchward's 1906 design for the initial 'Star' incorporated examples of the 'best practice' culled from France and the USA. The resulting locomotives were probably 20 years ahead of their competitors on other pre-Grouping lines and, as they were progressively developed by Churchward's successor Collett in the 1920s, provided for all the Great Western's express locomotive needs to the end of steam.

Lode Star was built at Swindon in February 1907. It ran over two million miles in service and was withdrawn in July 1951. On withdrawal it was decided that the locomotive should be exhibited in 1932 condition as this was the date most appropriate to the boiler and many of the existing fittings. The photograph shows yet another aspect of a National Collection locomotive's life — turning up in unusual locations. *Lode Star* was preserved in the Great Western Museum at Swindon from 1962 to 1992, but in 1992 it came to York to take its place in the refurbished Great Hall. The locomotive is seen 'under the wires' of the East Coast main line at York in March 1992. *NRM collection*

London, Tilbury & Southend Railway 4-4-2T
No 80 *Thundersley* (1909)

Above: Geographically, Thundersley is a village in southeast Essex — ironically not served by the London, Tilbury & Southend Railway! Mechanically, the locomotive is an example of an express passenger tank built by a private builder (Robert Stephenson & Co) for a line whose business was chiefly commuter traffic in and out of the metropolis.

Thundersley was withdrawn from service in 1956, having spent its latter years in the East Midlands. It was restored to working order at Derby in the same year and the restoration caused a number of criticisms in that LTSR livery sat uneasily on a locomotive which had been much modified — for example by the fitting of an extended smokebox sometime between 1915–20 — since its Tilbury days. The livery itself was regarded by many as NER 'Saxon' green rather than the true colour. The locomotive hauled special trains to celebrate the centenary of the LTSR and is seen here leaving Southend on 11 March 1956. After the celebrations the locomotive returned to Derby, spent a brief time in store at Hellifield and since 1968 has been on loan to Bressingham Railway Museum. *NRM collection/N. A. MacKillop*

North Eastern Railway Class T3 0-8-0 No 901 (1919)

Left: Built at Darlington in 1919, No 901 was the first of a class of 15 three-cylinder 0-8-0s. Reclassified 'Q7' by the LNER and eventually numbered 63460 by British Railways, the locomotive spent its life in the North East. In the 1950s the locomotive was fitted with Westinghouse air pumps to enable it to work the air-operated doors of the iron ore trains between Tyne Dock and Consett. It was withdrawn from service in December 1962 and was stored at Darlington Works pending preservation. The locomotive returned to rail tour duty in September 1963, successfully working a Stephenson Locomotive Society/Railway Correspondence and Travel Society five-day tour around the railway byways of North East England. The picture shows No 63460 in the course of this tour at Bishop Auckland. On final withdrawal in 1964 the locomotive was stored at Darlington, Stratford, Hellifield and Brighton before arriving in York in 1977. *J. S. Gilks*

Below: In 1978 the locomotive was placed in the custodianship of the North Eastern Locomotive Preservation Group and was finally returned to working order on the North Yorkshire Moors Railway in 1990. The picture shows LNER No 901 at Goathland in June 1991. *North Yorkshire Moors Railway*

Great Central Railway Class 11F 4-4-0
No 506 *Butler-Henderson* (1920)

Left: The inside-cylinder 4-4-0 was the characteristic express locomotive of the Edwardian age and five locomotives of this type are preserved as part of the National Collection.

One of the last designs was J. G. Robinson's 'Improved Director' of which *Butler-Henderson* was the first example. In LNER days these engines were considered worthy of development and a second series was built for use in Scotland. Here they received a series of esoteric names culled from the novels of Sir Walter Scott.

Butler-Henderson remained south of the border working trains on both the former Great Central and Great Northern routes. In British Railways days it became No 62660 and from 1957 wore a plain black livery — a far cry from the original Great Central green and maroon. *Butler-Henderson* is shown here on one of its later duties, a Derby to Lincoln train at Newark Castle in 1959. The locomotive was withdrawn from service in October 1960 having run 1,280,897 miles. *NRM collection*

Right: Having been withdrawn from service, *Butler-Henderson* was returned to 'original condition' and livery at Gorton Works. The locomotive was exhibited at Manchester Central goods station in March 1962 and in November 1962 was towed — by rail and over the former GC route! — to the museum at Clapham.

In 1975 *Butler-Henderson* was placed on loan to the Main Line Steam Trust on the Great Central Railway at Loughborough and in 1982 was returned to steam. As the locomotive came towards the end of its active life, it was repainted in British Railways black livery — lined on one side at least — and is seen here leaving Rothley station on 22 February 1992. The locomotive is now at York, restored again to Great Central livery. *Author's collection*

London & North Western Railway Class G2 0-8-0 No 485 (1921)

Left: It was a logical progression from the six-coupled (eg the 'Dean Goods') to the eight-coupled locomotive for heavy haulage. The picture, taken at the Midland Railway Centre at Butterley in February 1993, hints at the shape of things to come, as the 0-8-0, generally referred to as the 'Super D', is currently undergoing a long-term restoration at York.

No 485 was built at Crewe Works in 1921 at a cost of £8,900. No 49395 (British Railways numbering) was withdrawn from service at Buxton in November 1959. In its latter days, No 49395 had suffered 'irreparable' damage to cylinder block and motion caused by water 'carry over' from too high a level in the boiler. Modern engineering techniques and sponsorship monies are likely to overcome this 'irreparable' damage in the foreseeable future and the 'Super D', one of only four 'Premier line' tender locomotives in preservation, should steam again. *Robin Stewart-Smith*

North Staffordshire Railway 0-6-2T No 2 (1922)

Above: The NSR was one of the smaller pre-1923 companies, but a nonetheless important one. Much of its traffic was handled by tank engines, and the 'L' class 0-6-2Ts introduced in 1903 and built in batches up to 1923 provided it with some highly competent locomotives suitable for both passenger and freight work. When displaced by the LMSR's standardisation policy, five were purchased in 1936/7 by the Manchester Collieries Co Ltd for use on its extensive industrial railway system, later passing into NCB ownership. In 1960 one of these was restored to its original livery as NSR No 2 for the City of Stoke-on-Trent Golden Jubilee celebrations and remained in this livery for the rest of its NCB career. It is seen here at Walkden yard on 3 April 1965. *Alan Tyson*

31

Great Western Railway 'Castle' class 4-6-0
No 4073 *Caerphilly Castle* (1923)

Above: 'The first of a new class, to which larger cylinders and boilers and other improved features have been fitted. The increased capacity thus gained renders the locomotive capable of dealing with the heaviest and fastest trains, whilst retaining a margin of power in reserve.' Thus *The Railway Engineer* of October 1923 greeted the evolution of the 'Star' into the 'Castle' and the introduction of No 4073 *Caerphilly Castle*.

The locomotive, claimed as the most powerful in Britain based on tractive effort, was displayed at the Empire Exhibition in Wembley between April and October 1924 and amassed nearly two million miles in service. Exactly a year before withdrawal *Caerphilly Castle* is seen at Newport High Street station with train No 723, the 3.15pm ex-*Paddington* en route for Fishguard. *Colour-Rail BRW1109*

Right: Caerphilly Castle was withdrawn from service in May 1960. Being virtually as built apart from a few minor details, the locomotive was repainted at Swindon before being placed in the Science Museum.

In this evocative view taken on 4 June 1961, *Caerphilly Castle* is in the tender care of Messrs Pickfords as it is gently manoeuvred along All Saints Road in West London. The shop-frontages and traffic densities are a delight to behold!

In September 1996 this movement took place in reverse. In order to facilitate exhibition development within the Science Museum, *Caerphilly Castle* was removed from the Museum and placed in the hands of the Great Western Society at Didcot.
R. C. Riley

London, Midland & Scottish Railway Class 4F 0-6-0
No 4027 (1924)

Above: Locomotives of the 0-6-0 type were built by most companies in large numbers and the Midland Railway was no exception. With the 'Midlandisation' of LMS locomotive policy immediately after the Grouping, it would come as no surprise to find that the National Collection locomotive is in fact the first 'Derby 4' built for the LMS.

No 4027 cost £4,600 to construct at Derby Works. The only major alterations in the locomotive's appearance during its life have been the removal of the cylinder tail-rods and the substitution of a Stanier chimney for the original Fowler type.

The locomotive was withdrawn from Workington shed in November 1964. It was stored successively at Hellifield and Leicester before arriving at the Midland Railway Centre at Butterley. Restored to working order, No 4027 is seen here in the 'Rocket 150' parade at Rainhill on 24 May 1980. The locomotive is at present at Butterley undergoing restoration. *Hugh Ballantyne*

Southern Railway 'King Arthur' class 4-6-0
No 777 *Sir Lamiel* (1925)

Above: The consultative panel of the BTC Department of Historical Relics left the National Collection well endowed with express locomotives of the former Southern Railway, one of each type eventually being preserved.

It was intended to preserve the locomotive *King Arthur* but due to its poor condition when withdrawn *Sir Lamiel* was substituted in late 1961. The 'King Arthurs', a basic two-cylinder design, were developed from the 'N15' class 4-6-0s of the Southern's constituent, the London & South Western Railway. Robustly built, they proved efficient and trouble-free in service. *Sir Lamiel* was one of a batch known as 'Scotch Arthurs', having been delivered from the North British Locomotive Co Works in Glasgow in 1925. It was eventually returned to main line working order by the Humberside Locomotive Preservation Group in 1982. It is seen here, sporting Southern Railway olive green livery of the mid-1930s, passing Penyghent on the 'Long Drag' from Settle to Ribblehead with a 'SLOA Santa Special' on 27 December 1984. *Peter Zabek*

Left: It was an inspired move by the Southern Railway's publicity department to bestow on its newest express locomotives names from the Arthurian legends. *Sir Lamiel* seems to have been very much a lesser knight, described by Malory in *Morte d'Arthur* only as 'Sir Lamyell of Cardiff who was also a great lover'.

The mechanical knight's reputation seems to have been based on an exploit in 1936 which was described by the eminent locomotive historian Cecil J. Allen as 'probably the most astonishing example of "King Arthur" ability on the Southern Railway that has ever yet been seen'. *Sir Lamiel* ran from Salisbury to London, a distance of $83\frac{3}{4}$ miles, at an average speed of 69.2mph. Maximum speed was 90mph at Byfleet and the $33\frac{1}{2}$ miles from Worting Junction to Esher were covered at an average speed of 82.7mph. The locomotive gained $17\frac{3}{4}$ min on a 90min schedule with a load of 10 coaches.

Today's vogue in preservation is for 'just the way it was in the 1950s'. *Sir Lamiel*, now BR No 30777, stands in front of the depository at Stewarts Lane; familiar surroundings, but the date is 4 November 1994. *R. C. Riley*

Southern Railway 'Lord Nelson' class 4-6-0
No 850 *Lord Nelson* (1926)

Left: Lord Nelson is seen at Eastleigh in British Railways livery. The locomotive was withdrawn from service in August 1962 having run a distance of 1.3 million miles in service. After being stored at Stratford Works and Preston Park, the locomotive came to York in 1977 and was returned to working order at Carnforth in the period 1978-80. After a period of main line operation between 1980-86, the locomotive returned to Carnforth where at the time of writing it is now stored out of service.
Colour-Rail BRS703

Above: Designed by R. E. L. Maunsell, the 16 'Lord Nelson' class four-cylinder 4-6-0s were intended to haul heavy boat-trains to the South Coast at an average speed of 55mph. Impressive and powerful, their performance did not always match their looks until the class was fitted with the Lemaître exhaust system, by Maunsell's successor O. V. S. Bulleid, in the late 1930s. It is in this form that *Lord Nelson* is preserved and the above picture shows the locomotive in its period of active preservation leaving Wennington with the Carnforth to Hellifield leg of the 'Cumbrian Mountain Express' on 4 April 1981. *J. S. Gilks*

London, Midland & Scottish Railway Class 5MT 2-6-0 No 2700 (1926)

Left: Locomotive development until early in the 20th century had tended towards specific 'passenger' and 'freight' designs. However, by the 1900s the need increasingly arose for 'mixed traffic' engines which would be particularly suitable for the growing amount of fast freight and at the same time be at home on passenger duties other than the heaviest expresses. These locos were mainly of the 2-6-0 and 4-6-0 wheel arrangements and the only example in the National Collection of the former is the first of the LMS 2-6-0s designed and built at Horwich from 1926. Withdrawn in 1966, No 2700 had a brief spell of work on the Keighley & Worth Valley Railway in the late 1960s and is seen here crossing Mytholmes Viaduct on 3 November 1968. In their early days, preserved railways often adopted their own colour schemes for coaching stock before moving to authentic liveries. No 2700 has recently moved on loan to the East Lancashire Railway where it may be restored to working order again. *Robin Lush*

Great Western Railway 'King' class 4-6-0 No 6000 *King George V* (1927)

Above: Representing the final development of the GWR four-cylinder 4-6-0, the GWR 'Kings' were introduced in 1927, working the heaviest expresses to Bristol, the West of England and Wolverhampton. The doyen of the class, No 6000 *King George V*, now resides in the Great Western Railway Museum at Swindon. It is seen here at Chippenham on a running-in duty in July 1949, wearing the light blue livery which was one of the experimental colour schemes tried out by the new BR after Nationalisation. It has to be said that this did not go well with the brass and copper of GWR locos! *Colour-Rail BRW387*

Left: The livery finally adopted by BR for express locos was Brunswick green, based on the GWR style; *King George V* is in green in this view of it hauling a Wolverhampton-Paddington express and picking up water on Aynho troughs, south of Banbury, *c*1958. No 6000 now carries the double chimney fitted in 1956, while the bell was presented by the Baltimore & Ohio Railroad in 1927 to mark the engine's visit to the USA for the B&O centenary that year. *NRM/P. Ransome-Wallis collection*

Above: King George V was loaned in 1969 to H. P. Bulmer Ltd, the cider makers of Hereford, which had established an exhibition train of Pullman carriages. From the end of steam in 1968 BR had enforced a ban on the running of steam-hauled special trains, but on 2 October 1971 No 6000 became the first loco to breach the ban when it worked from Hereford to Birmingham on the first stage of a week-long trial tour. It is seen here near Pilning on the South Wales main line with the Bulmer's Pullmans and two BR Mk1 carriages. One of BR's concerns over the running of steam excursions was that of trespass by photographers and the omens in this scene were hardly encouraging; fortunately a much more responsible attitude now prevails and *King George V's* pioneer run paved the way for the current extensive main line programme. *J. S. Gilks*

Southern Railway 'Schools' class 4-4-0 No 925 *Cheltenham* (1934)

Left: The 'Schools' class 4-4-0s introduced in 1930 provided the SR with a versatile express locomotive for all except the heaviest duties and they were particularly suitable on the Hastings line which was afflicted by tunnels with restricted clearances. They were the most powerful 4-4-0s to run in Britain and proved capable of doing much of the work performed by larger engines such as the 'King Arthurs'. In its last two months of service No 30925 *Cheltenham* approaches Clayton Tunnel with an enthusiasts' special to Brighton on 7 October 1962. This was organised by the Railway Correspondence & Travel Society which was instrumental in influencing the choice of *Cheltenham* as the example to be preserved; the society had been founded in that town and used the locomotive as its logo. *Colour-Rail BRS845*

Right: Early in 1980 *Cheltenham* was restored to working order to run in the 'Rocket 150' cavalcade at Rainhill. It is seen here presenting a rather spectral appearance undergoing a steam test at the NRM in white primer prior to being finished in SR malachite green livery with its Southern number, 925. *NRM collection*

London, Midland & Scottish Railway Class 5 4-6-0
No 5000 (1935)

Above: The archetypical British mixed traffic locomotive must surely be the LMS Class 5 4-6-0, if only in terms of the number built (842) and the extent of the railway system over which they eventually worked. They had an outstanding reputation as 'go anywhere, do anything' engines and the planned first of the class, No 5000, (though not actually the first into service) has a deserved place in the NRM at the head of the Royal Train vehicles. It had survived in service until October 1967, only 10 months before the end of BR steam. In May 1980, whilst on loan to the Severn Valley Railway, it participated in the cavalcade at Rainhill marking the 150th anniversary of the Liverpool & Manchester Railway. *NRM collection*

London & North Eastern Railway Class V2
No 4771 *Green Arrow* (1936)

Above: Green Arrow was the first of an outstandingly successful class of high-speed mixed traffic locomotives introduced on to the LNER in 1936 by H. N. Gresley. The 'Green Arrow' service was the LNER's express parcels delivery and the locomotive was the prototype of the only British 2-6-2 tender locomotive design to go into series production.

The 'V2s' became known as 'the engines which won the war'. Their haulage capacity was prodigious and they tackled passenger and freight duties with an equally syncopated style.

Green Arrow was always a King's Cross engine, except for one month in 1953 when it was allocated to Woodford Halse on the former Great Central route. In BR days the locomotive was No 60800 and between 1949 and 1958 wore the incongruous British Railways lined black livery! By the time *Green Arrow* was listed for preservation in 1960 it was in BR green livery but remained substantially in 'as built' condition, particularly with regard to the original single casting for the three cylinders. Once the locomotive was withdrawn, in August 1962, it was most appropriate therefore that it should be put back into LNER livery and this was done at Doncaster in April 1963.

The picture shows *Green Arrow* on home ground with an up express at Grantham in August 1961. *Colour-Rail BRE798*

Above: Green Arrow was restored to working order at Norwich in 1972-73. Over 20 years of special steam service on the main line, No 4771 has proved to be one of the most economic and efficient performers of all the fleet of preserved locomotives. At the time of writing *Green Arrow* is undergoing a major overhaul in the Museum workshops with a view to a return to main line running.

The photographs show *Green Arrow* in preserved service, often far from its native heath. Here, *Green Arrow* approaches Appleby with a southbound 'Cumbrian Mountain Express' in May 1989. *Graham Maple*

Above: Green Arrow stands at Holyhead with a return 'North Wales Coast Express' bound for Crewe in August 1991. *Author's Collection*

London & North Eastern Railway Class A4 4-6-2
No 4468 *Mallard* (1938)

Above: When the LNER's 'A4' streamlined Pacifics appeared in 1935 for the high-speed services on the East Coast main line, their publicity value was immense and the new streamlined 'Silver Jubilee' service was a success from the start. No 4468 *Mallard* owes its selection as the National Collection's representative of an outstanding design to its performance on 3 July 1938 when, during the course of

braking trials, it established a new world speed record for steam traction of 126mph. In 1948, after Nationalisation, *Mallard* was one of the participants in a series of locomotive exchange trials for the new British Railways and is seen here leaving Waterloo station with the 'Atlantic Coast Express' on 8 June. It carries its later LNER number, 22, and the plaque fitted in 1947 to commemorate the speed record.
NRM/C. C. B. Herbert collection

Left: In 1985 *Mallard* was returned to steam in anticipation of the 50th anniversary of its record run in 1988. On 27 September 1985 on the 10th anniversary of the opening of the NRM it was steamed for the first time since 1963, still without its streamlined cladding. Alongside is an East Coast route 'flyer' of a previous generation, GNR 4-2-2 No 1, also in steam. *Author's collection*

Above: The 50th anniversary of the record run was celebrated on 3 July 1988 by a gathering of 'A4s' at York. *Mallard* was joined by No 4498 *Sir Nigel Gresley* and No 4464 *Bittern* masquerading as the pioneer member of the class, No 2509 *Silver Link*, and painted in the original silver-grey livery carried by the first four 'A4s'. *NRM collection*

Above: Mallard made a number of runs to Scarborough on the BR-operated 'Scarborough Spa Express' services and this was appropriate since Scarborough Borough Council had provided generous sponsorship towards the loco's overhaul. Seen here near Huttons Ambo on 3 September 1986, No 4468 shows off the full streamlining extending down over the wheels and motion. Throughout its preservation *Mallard* has been displayed in the condition in which it ran in 1938 on the record run; the anomaly is that it should not really carry the commemorative plaque which was not fitted until 10 years later! *J. S. Gilks*

London, Midland & Scottish Railway 'Coronation' class 4-6-2 No 46229 *Duchess of Hamilton* (1938)

Above: The LMS 'Coronation' 4-6-2s, introduced in 1938 for use on the West Coast main line between Euston and Glasgow, were arguably the most powerful Pacifics to run in Britain. In line with the fashion of the day, 10 of the first 15 (and a further 15 later) were turned out with a streamlined casing, including the NRM's example No 6229 *Duchess of Hamilton*. In 1939 the LMS sent a train of new carriages for the

'Coronation Scot' service to the World's Fair in New York, along with one of the latest batch of 'Coronation' locomotives. *Duchess of Hamilton* was the locomotive chosen but for publicity reasons exchanged names and numbers with the original member of the class, No 6220 *Coronation*. In this guise it is seen at Flushing Meadow on 30 April 1939, in a rare prewar colour photograph, at the start of the World's Fair and after completing a 3,000-mile exhibition tour from Baltimore. It is fitted with a headlight and bell as required by USA regulations. *Paul Lubliner collection*

Left: Duchess of Hamilton returned to Britain in 1942, its stay in the USA unexpectedly prolonged due to the outbreak of war, and was restored to its correct identity, while by 1948 it had lost its streamlined casing as had all streamlined members of the class. For most of the 1950s it carried the standard BR green livery and is seen in this form, with its BR number, 46229, at Willesden depot in 1957. *Colour-Rail BRM455*

*Above:*In 1958 *Duchess of Hamilton* became one of 16 of the class to be given a new crimson lake livery based on the LMS colour scheme. No 46229 is seen here in non-too-clean condition heading the 'Lakes Express' between Lancaster and Hest Bank on 31 August 1962. *Colour-Rail BRM1172*

Left: After withdrawal in 1964, *Duchess of Hamilton* was preserved by Butlins Ltd at its Minehead Holiday Camp before being loaned to the NRM in 1975. In 1980 it was restored to working order with the aid of funds from a limited edition print and from the Friends of the NRM and in 1987 it was formally purchased by the Museum. A feature of main line operations with No 46229 in the early 1980s was the '55 Club' using the Museum's pair of 1960 Metro-Cammell Pullman cars in which a full meal service was provided for passengers at their seats. This pioneered the now commonplace 'upmarket' type of railway excursion with on-board catering. No 46229 arrives at Chester on 23 October 1982 with the Pullmans and Royal Train brake No 5155 as support vehicle. *Hugh Ballantyne*

Southern Railway Class Q1 0-6-0 No C1 (1942)

Above: The ultimate development of the classic British inside-cylinder 0-6-0 tender locomotive must have come as quite a shock when it appeared in 1942. The 'no frills' design reflected wartime austerity but in service the 'Charlies' (as they were known) proved to be powerful and effective.

The C1 numbering reflected the policies of the Southern's Chief Engineer, O. V. S. Bulleid. In 1948 under British Railways the locomotive became No 33001. Withdrawn in 1964, No 33001 was stored at Stratford Works and Preston Park, Brighton, before, in 1977, being placed jointly on loan to the Bulleid Society and the Bluebell Railway at Sheffield Park. The locomotive was overhauled and ran regularly between 1980–83. After a further lengthy overhaul the locomotive returned to service in September 1992 in the guise of Southern Railway No C1. It is seen here approaching Horsted Keynes — but is the year 1992 or 1942?
Dave Smith — Bluebell Railway

Southern Railway 'Battle of Britain' class 4-6-2
No 21C151 *Winston Churchill* (1946)

Above: The British Transport Commission intended to preserve one of O. V. S. Bulleid's smaller, yet no less innovative, Pacifics and it was appropriate that the locomotive which eventually came into the National Collection was the one to bear the name of perhaps the country's most charismatic Prime Minister.

The locomotive, numbered 21C151 in Bulleid's idiosyncratic styling, was delivered from Brighton Works in December 1946. It was named at Waterloo in September 1947 by Marshal of the Royal Air Force Lord Dowding, Churchill himself

not being present at the ceremony. On 30 January 1965 the locomotive hauled Sir Winston Churchill's funeral train from Waterloo to Handborough (Oxfordshire) via Richmond, Ascot, Reading, Didcot and Oxford, and the photograph shows this train. The second vehicle is bogie luggage van No S2464 which was used to convey the coffin.

The locomotive was withdrawn from service in September 1965 and placed in store in Brighton. From 1977 to 1984 it was at the Great Western Society's depot at Didcot; *Winston Churchill* arrived at York in September 1983 and is at present on display at the Museum's workshops. *Colour-Rail BRS181*

British Railways (Southern Region) 'Merchant Navy' class 4-6-2 No 35029 *Ellerman Lines* (1949)

Above: O. V. S. Bulleid's original 'Merchant Navy' Pacifics were remarkable machines. Technically remarkable in that they featured welded steel fireboxes with thermic syphons, chain-driven valve gear enclosed in an oil sump and 'air-smoothed' casings; remarkable also in that Bulleid managed to get these complicated express passenger machines built in the midst of wartime! Locomotives of this type continued to be built after Nationalisation; *Ellerman Lines* was constructed at Eastleigh in February 1949 and named in March 1951.

It was not intended to preserve a 'Merchant Navy' in the National Collection. *Ellerman Lines* was withdrawn from service in September 1966 and found its way to the 'elephants' graveyard of steam' — Barry. With the setting up of the National Railway Museum in York it was decided that a sectioned locomotive would be a valuable interpretive tool and *Ellerman Lines* was chosen for this role. The locomotive was sectioned by Flying Scotsman Enterprises at Market Overton in 1974.

The photograph shows *Ellerman Lines* in palmier days, at Stewarts Lane in October 1951 having just brought up the 'Night Ferry' from Dover.
Colour-Rail BRS380

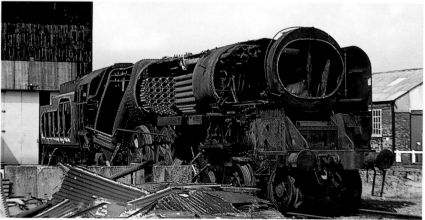

Above: In order to facilitate maintenance and to encourage more predictable performances, the 'Merchant Navies' were rebuilt into a simplified form in the 1950s. *Ellerman Lines* was so treated in September 1959 and makes a handsome sight heading the down 'Bournemouth Belle' through Esher in January 1962. *Geoff Rixon*

Left: Ellerman Lines in process of 'sectioning' at Market Overton in 1974. It is interesting to speculate on whether the locomotive in its present form receives more attention and comment than it ever did whilst at the head of the 'Bournemouth Belle'! *NRM collection*

British Railways Class EM1 (Class 76) Bo-Bo Electric No 26020 (1951)

Above: By September 1939, the work of converting the Manchester-Sheffield-Wath lines of the LNER to electric operation on the 1,500V dc overhead system was well in hand. However, war intervened and work was not completed, along with the boring of a new Woodhead Tunnel, until June 1954. Britain's first fully electrified main line for goods and passenger traffic was thus inaugurated.

Locomotive No 26020 was always something of a celebrity. Built at Gorton in 1951, it had already been exhibited at the Festival of Britain before, as seen in the photograph, it hauled the first official train through the new tunnel. Locomotives of this type hauled both passenger and freight trains on the route and the original locomotive, No 26000 *Tommy*, had spent the period between 1947 and 1952 in the Netherlands and was the first electric locomotive to run on Netherlands Railways.

The Woodhead route closed to all through traffic in 1981. No 26020, representing the perceived standard of main line electrification (1,500V dc) of the 1950s, had been withdrawn from service in 1977. It was repainted in British Railways black livery and displayed at York in 1978 in time for the Centenary of Electric Traction Exhibition a year later. *Colour-Rail DE1203*

British Railways 'Britannia' 4-6-2 No 70013 *Oliver Cromwell* (1951)

Above: After Nationalisation BR decided to build a range of new 'Standard' steam locomotives as electrification was a longer-term objective and the importing of fuel for the adoption of diesel traction was, in the postwar years, seen as too costly. The Class 7 'Britannia' 4-6-2s were introduced in 1951 and the prototype of the class, No 70000 *Britannia*, was originally scheduled for preservation. The choice was later changed to No 70013 *Oliver Cromwell* which, in 1967, became the last steam locomotive to be given a full overhaul by BR. No 70013 is working hard on the climb past Shap Quarry with a Carlisle–Blackpool football special on a cold Boxing Day 1967. *Colour-Rail BRM1284*

Above: After withdrawal of the remaining members of the class at the end of 1967, No 70013 was kept in service for excursion duties during the last months of steam on BR. One such was on 17 March 1968 when it arrived at Carnforth with a Williams Deacon's Bank Club special from Stockport. Five months later it took part in hauling the so-called 'Last BR Steam Train', since when it has been on loan to the Bressingham Steam Museum in Norfolk. *John Corkill*

British Railways Type 1 (Class 20) Bo-Bo Diesel-Electric No D8000 (1957)

Above: One aspect of the 1955 Modernisation Plan foresaw the gradual replacement of steam by diesel and electric traction. D8000 was the very first locomotive delivered under the Plan, built at the Vulcan Foundry of English Electric. It was allocated to the first all-diesel depot at Devons Road, Bow, in June 1957.

The picture shows D8000 undergoing braking trials on the Ilkeston branch in August 1957, shortly before it was displayed at the annual Derby Works Open Day. The original oval buffers and inspection steps can be easily seen in the photograph and the 'steam age' bonnet-forward aspect is obvious.

Under the modern traction renumbering scheme No D8000 became, in February 1974, a unit of Class 20, No 20050. It was withdrawn from service in December 1980 and eventually cosmetically restored at Doncaster Works. In 1994 moves to return No D8000 to working order at York were made when the Museum replaced the engine unit with a fully operable one from another Class 20. This process is on-going at time of writing. *Colour-Rail DE1656*

British Railways Class E5000 (Class 71) Bo-Bo Electric No E5001 (1958)

Right: The completion of electrification to the Kent Coast and the replacement of steam traction called for the provision of a class of powerful electric locomotives for freight traffic and to haul the prestige expresses such as the 'Golden Arrow' and the 'Night Ferry'.

No E5001, drawing current at 750V dc from either third-rail or overhead equipment, was delivered to traffic from Doncaster Works in January 1959.

In the British Rail renumbering these locomotives became Class 71 and E5001 metamorphosed into No 71001 in 1974. The locomotive was withdrawn from service in November 1977 and restored to its original green livery at Doncaster before being exhibited at York in the Centenary of Electric Traction Exhibition. In the summer of 1992 E5001 was restored to main line condition at Ashford and has since been active on the third-rail system of the former Southern Region.

The photograph shows E5001 at Longhedge Junction on 26 July 1959 in charge of a Luton to Margate excursion. *R. C. Riley*

British Railways Type 4 (Class 40) No D200 (1958)

Above: The BR Modernisation Plan pointed the way to the replacement of steam by diesel traction, at least where electrification was not feasible, and a 'Pilot Scheme' was introduced to test various types. Ten locos in the 'Type 4' power range (2,000–3,000hp) were delivered from English Electric in 1958, the first being No D200 (which is thus two years older than BR's last steam locomotive *Evening Star*!). The class eventually totalled 200 and later became BR Class 40. In its final years No D200/40 122 was repainted in its original livery and is seen here passing Duncowfold, south of Carlisle. It entered the NRM in 1988. *J. S. Gilks*

British Railways Class 9F 2-10-0 No 92220 *Evening Star* (1960)

Above: Evening Star is unique; the only steam locomotive built for Britain's railways to be marked down for official preservation from the moment it was constructed. Named with appropriate ceremony at Swindon Works on 18 March 1960, *Evening Star* was withdrawn from service in March 1965 after running a mere 130,000 miles, a mileage which in actual fact can hardly have given any return on the initial investment of £33,497.

The Class 9Fs were probably the most successful of the British Railways standard designs. They proved highly versatile as well as being the ultimate in British heavy freight locomotive design. *Evening Star* spent the majority of her working life allocated to Cardiff Canton depot. The locomotive is seen here, not quite living up to celebrity status, passing through Oxford with a modest freight in August 1964.
Joe Richardson

Above: Although intended for freight duties, the Class 9Fs proved to be speedy machines and occasionally were pressed into service on passenger trains. Their small driving wheels proved no handicap and *Evening Star* is recorded as performing creditably on express service between Cardiff and London. In the summers of 1960-62 a number of '9Fs' worked holiday traffic on the undulating Somerset & Dorset route between Bath Green Park and Bournemouth West. They proved popular on the heavy trains and *Evening Star* was allocated to the route in August 1962. It is seen here on 8 September 1962 climbing towards Devonshire Tunnel with the last Manchester-Bournemouth 'Pines Express' over the original Somerset & Dorset route. *Colour-Rail SD93*

Right: Evening Star was withdrawn from service, 'nicely run in' in 1965. She was repaired at Crewe in 1967 and stored at Preston Park, Brighton, from 1968 until 1973 when the locomotive was lent for operation on the Keighley & Worth Valley Railway. *Evening Star* joined the Museum collection at York in 1975 and appeared at both the 150th anniversary celebrations for the Stockton & Darlington and Liverpool & Manchester Railways in 1975 and 1980 respectively. The locomotive operated at regular intervals on main line steam specials and made popular visits to preserved railways such as the West Somerset and the North Yorkshire Moors. The locomotive returned to York in 1991 and at present is an integral part of the locomotive display with no thought of a return to steam.

The picture shows *Evening Star* approaching Goathland station on the North Yorkshire Moors Railway with a through working from Whitby in October 1987. *Colour-Rail P230*

British Railways Type 5 (Class 55) Co-Co No 55002
The King's Own Yorkshire Light Infantry (1961)

Above: The 'Deltic' diesel-electrics proved an outstanding success on the East Coast main line from their introduction in 1961. By 1970 they had brought the best London-Newcastle timing down to 3hr 35min, an improvement of an hour on the best steam times. By the 1980s, however, they were being displaced from the principal expresses by the new 'InterCity 125' High Speed Trains and withdrawal of the class was completed in 1981. Although the prototype *Deltic* was already in the collection, it was felt appropriate to acquire an example of the production run as well, thus completing the Museum's remarkable range of East Coast route express motive power. No 55002 (originally D9002) *The King's Own Yorkshire Light Infantry* was selected and in 1980 the Friends of the NRM sponsored its repainting in its original two-tone green livery, though with full yellow 'visibility' ends. No 55002 stands at York station during 1981 alongside one of the HSTs which usurped it. *NRM collection*

British Railways Type 4 (Class 50) Co-Co
No 50033 *Glorious* (1968)

*Above:*With the trend towards fixed-formation train units with power cars, the English
Electric Class 50s might well be Britain's last express passenger diesel-electric
locomotives. Introduced in 1967, they were initially used on the West Coast main line
north of Crewe, often in pairs to accelerate schedules, later migrating to the Western
Region once the West Coast route had been electrified through to Glasgow, while in
their later years they became associated with the ex-LSWR Waterloo-Exeter line.
The WR bestowed on the class a series of stirring names mostly based on naval
heritage; the SR's legacy was to bedeck its allocation in the eye-catching 'Network
South East' livery. No 50033 *Glorious* (originally No D433) heads along the scenic
coastal stretch of the West of England main line at Shaldon Bridge, near Teignmouth,
with a Paignton-Waterloo train in September 1991. Withdrawal of the Class 50s was
completed in 1994. *Colour-Rail DE1482*

British Railways Advanced Passenger Train — Experimental (1972)

Left: The APT programme was a gallant attempt to provide a high speed train service without actually rebuilding many of Britain's sinuous pioneer main lines.

The Experimental train featured two gas-turbine engined power cars and two trailer cars. The latter were packed with scientific instruments to monitor the performance of the tilting mechanisms and the hydro-kinetic braking systems — designed to stop a 150mph train in the signalling distances allowed for the more traditional 100mph variety.

Tests proved promising and a passenger-carrying APT was authorised, APT-P (P for prototype). This made its first passenger-carrying run in December 1981 but proved unsuccessful and was withdrawn in 1986.

APT-E came to the Museum in 1976; the picture shows it, hopefully posed, on the test track at Old Dalby in Leicestershire. *NRM collection*

British Railways Experimental Railbus LEV-1 (1978)

Right: Designed jointly by the research divisions of British Railways and Leyland Vehicles, LEV-1 took to the rails in 1978. Formed of two Leyland bus bodies on a specially designed two-axle underframe, it was designed to be a modern lightweight railbus for branch lines and proved to be the progenitor of the 'Pacer' family of two and three-car units.

After initial trials LEV-1 was shipped to the USA and ran on the rural lines of New England. These trials were successful enough for a number of units were ordered for service overseas.

On its return to Britain LEV-1 saw service between Ipswich and Lowestoft in the winter of 1980-1. The picture shows it awaiting departure from Ipswich on 28 November 1980.

After this service LEV-1 was used for research purposes. On 16 July 1983 it ran at the 'Railbus Silver Jubilee' on the Keighley & Worth Valley Railway and was acquired by the Museum in 1987. A Mk3 LEV was purchased by Northern Ireland Railways for service on the Coleraine-Portrush branch and is now preserved at the Ulster Folk & Transport Museum, Cultra. *J. S. Gilks*

BR 350hp Class 08 0-6-0 No 13079 (1954)

Right: The humble shunting locomotive has always been one of the railways' unsung heroes; however, three diesel shunters in the collection not only represent this traction development but also play an active and important part in the NRM's life as working shunters around its two sites. The most powerful of these is the BR/English Electric Class 08, an outstandingly successful diesel-electric locomotive which goes back to an LMS design of 1944. The LNER, GWR and SR all had similar machines and after nationalisation their details were brought together into the design which went into production in 1952, with over 1,000 being built, and which has survived to be the standard shunting locomotive to this day. The design was also developed for export and examples can be seen in use overseas, notably in the Netherlands. No 13079 was built at BR's Darlington Works in 1954; later renumbered D3079 and 08064, it was withdrawn in 1984 and has been restored to its original livery and number. *NRM collection*

BR 170hp Class 02 0-4-0 No D2860 (1961)

Below: Many goods yards and docks sidings required shunting locomotives with a short wheelbase to negotiate their sharp curves and points and this situation saw many long-lived pre-Grouping steam designs still in use by the start of the 1960s. In 1960 the Yorkshire Engine Co of Sheffield produced this diesel-hydraulic design, powered by a Rolls-Royce engine, but the closure of many of these goods yards meant that the class was destined for only a brief life on BR, with withdrawals commencing in 1969 although several examples were sold for industrial use. No D2860 was withdrawn in 1970 and stored until 1978 when it was refurbished by Thomas Hill (Rotherham) Ltd for active preservation at the NRM. *NRM collection*

Liverpool & Manchester Railway 0-2-2 *Rocket* (Reproduction 1979)

Right: The remains of the original *Rocket*, built to win the Rainhill Trials of 1829, were presented to the Patent Office Museum, the predecessor of today's Science Museum, in 1862. Replicas of arguably the world's most famous steam locomotive were built at the time of the centenary and sesquicentenary of the first 'inter-city' railway, the Liverpool & Manchester.

At the time of the centenary a working reproduction of the locomotive was built, by the Robert Stephenson Co, for Henry Ford's Greenfield Village Museum at Dearborn in the USA. In 1934 a sectioned locomotive, also built by Robert Stephenson's, was placed in the Science Museum. This locomotive is now at York.

The 1979 locomotive was built for the Museum by Locomotive Enterprises of Springwell, Tyne and Wear, under the direction of the late Mike Satow. It is seen here, undergoing steaming tests, at Springwell in the spring of 1979. This *Rocket* was intended to be the 'star' of the 'Rocket 150' celebrations, held at Rainhill in 1980 to celebrate the 150th anniversary of the Liverpool & Manchester. *NRM collection*

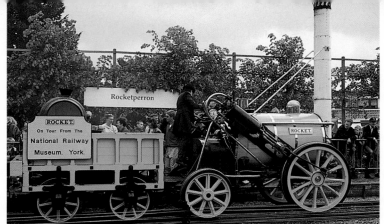

Left: After its appearance at the 'Rocket 150' celebrations in 1980, the reproduction *Rocket* became something of a talisman for the National Railway Museum. The locomotive was much in demand at railway museums and associated railway events all over the world, and has represented the Museum in the USA, Australia, Japan, France, Germany, the Netherlands and the Czech Republic. The main picture shows *Rocket* at 'The Great Railway Exposition' in Osaka, Japan, in March 1983. The locomotive created tremendous interest in Japan and to reach this venue *Rocket* became the first steam locomotive to fly over the North Pole — albeit in the cargo hold of a 'Jumbo' jet. *Author's collection*

Above: The smaller picture shows *Rocket* at the second National Steam Festival at the Netherlands Railway Museum in Utrecht in May 1996. The fostering of international links with sister museums is an important use of the reproduction locomotive. *Author's collection*

Right: The reproduction *Rocket* is also widely travelled within the British Isles. The locomotive is used as part of the Museum's 'outreach' programme visiting preserved railways, railway works, open days and other museums. It is also used as part of the Museum's marketing initiatives and in this role visits events such as county shows. At York the locomotive is used for demonstration and dramatic purposes.

The picture shows *Rocket* running into Castle Hedingham station on the Colne Valley Railway in Essex. The locomotive has visited the Colne Valley twice, in October 1988 and September 1991, on both occasions to take part in the railway's acclaimed Victorian Festival for local schools.

The reproduction *Rocket* portrays the locomotive at the time that it won the Rainhill Trials. Modern safety requirements demand that the new locomotive carries a welded boiler, modern safety-valve, steel driving wheels and an efficient air-brake system. To all external intents and purposes, however, today's *Rocket* looks and performs very much as did the original. *Author's collection*

Great Western Railway 4-2-2
Iron Duke (Broad Gauge Reproduction 1985)

Above: When the National Railway Museum was set up in 1975 one of the most significant gaps in the collection was the lack of a representative locomotive from the 'broad gauge' (7ft 0¼in) of Brunel's Great Western Railway. This gap was filled by the building by the Science Museum in 1985 of a reproduction of the locomotive *Iron Duke* of 1847. So successful were the original 'Iron Dukes' that locomotives of the same basic design continued to be the mainstay of broad gauge expresses until the demise of the gauge in 1892.

Elegant though the reproduction *Iron Duke* is, most of the working parts, boiler,

cylinders, motion and the like, come from the former Hunslet 'Austerity' 0-6-0 saddle tanks donated by the former National Coal Board. The *Iron Duke* project was overseen by Tony Hall-Patch of the Science Museum, the locomotive being constructed by Resco Railways of Woolwich and the tender by British Rail Workshops at Cathays, Cardiff.

Iron Duke is seen here in the South Yard of the National Railway Museum during the Museum's 10th anniversary celebrations in September 1985. A diminutive *Rocket* lurks in the distance! *Author's collection*

Above: Maximum gauge — minimum gauge! *Iron Duke* was completed at Easter 1985 in time to inaugurate the celebrations for the 150th anniversary of the founding of the Great Western Railway. These celebrations proved to be somewhat ill-fated but in September 1985 *Iron Duke* appeared, most appropriately, at an open weekend at the motive power depot at Old Oak Common.

One of the reasons for the commissioning of the *Iron Duke* reproduction was to show the sheer size of the Great Western broad gauge. This is particularly noticeable here as *Iron Duke* stands alongside the 15in gauge Pacific *Green Goddess* of the Romney, Hythe & Dymchurch Railway at the Old Oak Common event. Britain's widest and narrowest practicable gauges are interpreted to some effect!

In action *Iron Duke* is a magnificent sight. It is to be regretted that only two very short lengths of broad gauge track exist in the country — at York and at the Great Western Society depot at Didcot — and that *Iron Duke* cannot be given his head. *Author's collection*

Locomotives in the National Collection

Date	Description	Location
Steam		
1813	Wylam Colliery 0-4-0 *Puffing Billy*	Science Museum
1822	Hetton Colliery 0-4-0	North of England Open Air Museum, Beamish
1825	S&DR 0-4-0 No 1 *Locomotion*	North Road Museum, Darlington
1829	Shutt End Colliery 0-4-0 *Agenoria*	National Railway Museum
1829	L&MR 0-2-2 *Rocket*	Science Museum
1829	L&MR 0-4-0 *Sans Pareil*	Science Museum
1829	L&MR 0-2-2 *Novelty*	Manchester Museum of Science & Industry
1845	S&DR 0-6-0 No 25 *Derwent*	North Road Museum, Darlington
1845	LNWR 2-2-2 No 1868 *Columbine*	National Railway Museum
1846	Furness Railway 0-4-0 No 3 *Coppernob*	National Railway Museum
1847	LNWR 2-2-2 No 3020 *Cornwall*	The Railway Age, Crewe
1857	Wantage Tram 0-4-0WT No 5 *Shannon* (formerly *Jane*)	The Great Western Society, Didcot
1865	LNWR 0-4-0ST *Pet*	National Railway Museum
1865	LNWR 0-4-0ST No 1439	East Lancs Railway
1866	MR 2-4-0 No 158A	Midland Railway Centre, Butterley
1868	SDR 0-4-0T No 151 *Tiny*	South Devon Railway
1869	NER 2-2-4T No 66 *Aerolite*	National Railway Museum
1870	GNR 4-2-2 No 1	National Railway Museum
1874	LSWR 2-4-0WT No 298	South Devon Railway
1874	Hebburn Works 0-4-0ST No 2 *Bauxite*	National Railway Museum
1874	NER 0-6-0 No 1275	National Railway Museum
1875	NER 2-4-0 No 910	North Road Museum, Darlington
1880	LBSCR 0-6-0T No 82 *Boxhill*	National Railway Museum
1882	LBSCR 0-4-2 No 214 *Gladstone*	National Railway Museum
1885	NER 2-4-0 No 1463	North Road Museum, Darlington
1887	L&YR 0-4-0ST *Wren*	National Railway Museum
1889	L&YR 2-4-2T No 1008	National Railway Museum
1892	LNWR 2-4-0 No 790 *Hardwicke*	National Railway Museum
1893	S&MR 0-4-2WT *Gazelle*	Col Stephens Railway Museum, Tenterden
1893	LSWR 4-4-0 No 563	National Railway Museum
1893	NER 4-4-0 No 1621	National Railway Museum
1894	GER 2-4-0 No 490	Bressingham Steam Museum
1897	LSWR 0-4-4T 'M7' class No 245	National Railway Museum
1897	GWR 0-6-0 No 2516	Great Western Museum, Swindon
1897	Taff Vale Railway 0-6-2T No 28	Dean Forest Railway
1898	GNR 4-4-2 No 990 *Henry Oakley*	Steamtown Railway Museum, Carnforth
1899	MR 4-2-2 No 673	National Railway Museum
1899	GNR 0-6-0ST 'J52' class No 1247	East Somerset Railway
1899	LSWR 4-4-0 'T9' class No 120	Bluebell Railway
1901	SECR 4-4-0 No 737	National Railway Museum
1902	MR 4-4-0 No 1000	National Railway Museum
1902	GNR 4-4-2 No 251	National Railway Museum
1903	GWR 4-4-0 No 3440 *City of Truro*	Great Western Museum, Swindon
1904	GER 0-6-0T No 87	National Railway Museum
1905	GER 0-6-0 'J17' class No 1217	National Railway Museum
1905	GWR 2-8-0 '28xx' class No 2818	National Railway Museum
1907	GWR 4-6-0 No 4003 *Lode Star*	National Railway Museum
1909	LTSR 4-4-2T No 80 *Thundersley*	Bressingham Steam Museum
1911	GCR 2-8-0 Class 04 No 102	Great Central Railway
1919	NER 0-8-0 'Q7' class No 901	North Yorkshire Moors Railway
1920	GCR 4-4-0 'Director' class No 506 *Butler-Henderson*	National Railway Museum
1921	LNWR 0-8-0 'G2' class No 485	National Railway Museum
1922	NSR 0-6-2T No 2	North Staffs Railway
1923	GWR 4-6-0 'Castle' class No 4073 *Caerphilly Castle*	Great Western Society, Didcot
1924	LMSR 0-6-0 '4F' class No 4027	Midland Railway Centre, Butterley
1925	GWR 2-2-2 *North Star* (Broad Gauge Replica)	Great Western Museum, Swindon
1925	SR 4-6-0 'King Arthur' class No 777 *Sir Lamiel*	Great Central Railway
1926	SR 4-6-0 No 850 *Lord Nelson*	Steamtown Railway Museum, Carnforth
1926	LMSR 2-6-0 No 2700	East Lancs Railway
1927	GWR 4-6-0 'King' class No 6000 *King George V*	Great Western Museum, Swindon
1934	SR 4-4-0 'Schools' class No 925 *Cheltenham*	National Railway Museum
1934	LMSR 2-6-4T No 2500	Bressingham Steam Museum
1935	Chinese Govt Railways 4-8-4 'KF7' class No 607	National Railway Museum
1935	LMSR 4-6-0 No 5000	National Railway Museum
1936	LNER 2-6-2 'V2' class No 4771 *Green Arrow*	National Railway Museum
1938	LNER 4-6-2 'A4' class No 4468 *Mallard*	National Railway Museum
1938	LMSR 4-6-2 'Coronation' class No 46229 *Duchess of Hamilton*	National Railway Museum
1942	SR 0-6-0 'Q1' class No C1	Bluebell Railway
1942	Robert Stephenson & Hawthorn 0-4-0ST No 7063 (CEGB No 15) *Eustace Forth*	National Railway Museum
1945	SR 4-6-2 'Battle of Britain' class No 34051 *Winston Churchill*	National Railway Museum
1947	GWR 0-6-0PT No 9400	Great Western Museum, Swindon
1949	SR 4-6-2 Rebuilt 'Merchant Navy' class No 35029 *Ellerman Lines* (Sectioned)	National Railway Museum
1951	BR 4-6-2 'Britannia' class No 70013 *Oliver Cromwell*	Bressingham Steam Museum